Pelicans
Soaring the Seas

Frankie Stout

PowerKiDS press.
New York

To my cats, who are all cool

Published in 2009 by The Rosen Publishing Group, Inc.
29 East 21st Street, New York, NY 10010

First Edition

Editor: Nicole Pristash
Book Design: Kate Laczynski
Photo Researcher: Jessica Gerweck

Photo Credits: Cover, p. 1 © www.istockphoto.com/Thomas ONeil; pp. 5, 7, 15, 17, 19, 21 Shutterstock.com; p. 9 © www.istockphoto.com/Paul Tessier; p. 11 © Joseph Van Os/Getty Images, Inc.; p. 13 © Eastcott Momatiuk/Getty Images, Inc.

Library of Congress Cataloging-in-Publication Data

Stout, Frankie.
   Pelicans : soaring the seas / by Frankie Stout. — 1st ed.
      p. cm. — (Things with wings)
   Includes index.
   ISBN 978-1-4042-4497-9 (library binding)
   1. Pelicans—Juvenile literature. I. Title.
   QL696.P47S78 2009
   598.4'3—dc22

                                                2008007516

Manufactured in the United States of America

CONTENTS

Pelicans Are Things with Wings

Have you ever seen a pelican **soaring** through the air? Pelicans are large birds that live near water. There are many different kinds of pelicans, such as great white pelicans, brown pelicans, and pink-backed pelicans. Pelicans have strong, short legs with feet made for swimming. However, because their legs are short, pelicans are not good walkers.

Pelicans are great fliers, though. They have big wings, which let them fly high and nest in tall trees. A pelican's wings help it keep safe and help it find food. There are many other fun things to learn about pelicans. Let's find out more!

There are eight species, or types, of pelicans on Earth. The pelicans shown here are great white pelicans, which live in Eastern Europe, Africa, and Asia.

Pouches and Webs

Pelicans are unique, or special, because they have very long and interesting bills. These bills have large pouches under them made of skin. Pelicans use these pouches to get food. As the pelican fills up its pouch with seawater, the pouch also picks up fish, **shrimp**, and other foods. The water then **drains** from the pouch and the pelican can swallow the food it caught.

Pelicans have feet that are great for swimming. Their feet are webbed. This means that pelicans have skin between their toes. Webbed feet work like paddles, helping pelicans move around in the water.

The Australian pelican can have a bill up to 16 inches (41 cm) long. This is the longest bill of any bird in the world.

These Wings Are Made for Flying

Pelicans have very large wings. To soar, a pelican uses its big, strong wings to ride **currents** of air. This makes the pelican look as if it is floating. Pelicans soar so high in the sky that sometimes you cannot even see them!

The brown pelican, which lives in North America, uses its wings to dive from the air into the water. The brown pelican soars above the water in search of food. When the pelican sees some fish, it dives down to catch its next dinner in its pouch. A pelican needs its wings to stay living.

The brown pelican is the only type of pelican that dives for its food. When the pelican spots a fish, it will fly headfirst into the water.

Places for Pelicans

You can find pelicans in many places, such as Africa, Europe, Asia, Australia, and the Americas. Pelicans are found along coasts and near lakes, **swamps**, and other **wetlands**. They generally like to be where it is warm. This is why you will never find a pelican in Antarctica!

Pelicans like to live near water so that they can find their food very easily. Like many animals, its home is important to a pelican. Pelicans have been able to get used to many changes to their **habitats**. However, pelicans are in danger if their habitats become **polluted**.

These pelicans are walking in a wetland in Kenya, Africa. Wetlands are a good place for pelicans to live because wetlands are rich with water and food.

Together, One and All

Pelicans like to stay together. They like to feed and fly in groups. When it is time to have babies, pelicans form colonies. A colony is a group of the same kind of animals. A pelican colony can have thousands of pelicans in it.

Pelicans build their nests mostly out of sticks. Some of these nests are built high up in trees. **Male** and **female** pelicans build their nests together. The male pelican brings grass and sticks. Then the female shapes the nest.

Other pelicans do not build nests in trees. Instead, these pelicans make their homes on rocks.

This is a pelican colony at Lake Nakuru, in Africa. About 450 types of birds live around there.

Fishy Feeders

Pelicans like to eat. Great white pelicans, for example, can eat up to four large fish a day. Pelicans eat all kinds of fish, both big and small. Pelicans also eat frogs and other small water animals.

Hungry pelicans often hunt for food in groups. These pelicans help each other get their next dinner. Great white pelicans are group hunters. A group of great white pelicans will first make fish swim to **shallow** water, where it is easier to catch the fish. Then, the great white pelicans catch the fish and eat them whole in one big bite!

This great white pelican made its huge pouch big enough for it to swallow a fish whole!

Danger for Pelicans

Pelicans like to eat food, but they also have to try not to become food themselves! Luckily, adult pelicans do not have many **predators**. Pelicans are such good fliers and swimmers that not many animals can keep up with them. However, baby pelicans do have predators. Some animals, such as seagulls and crows, kill baby pelicans.

Sometimes a pelican will leave its eggs if people get too close and scare it. This means that the eggs will never have a chance to **hatch**. For this reason, you should never go near a pelican's nest. This will keep the eggs safe.

This seagull has a strong bill with a point at the end of the bill. This makes it easy for the seagull to break open and eat a pelican egg.

Time for Babies!

Pelicans lay one to three eggs per year. Many pelicans have their babies in the spring. However, in warmer places, pelicans can have babies all year long.

Baby pelicans are born without feathers. If they hatch on the ground, it can take a month for them to start walking. Babies that hatch in nests high off the ground can take two months to learn to fly.

Pelicans feed their babies by opening their bills wide. The chicks reach high into the parent's mouth to get their food. Chicks sometimes even fight each other for food from their mother and father!

This brown pelican is taking care of its babies in its nest. Soon the baby pelicans will grow feathers. Then the babies will be able to leave their nest and fly on their own.

Dalmatian Pelicans

One kind of pelican stands out among the rest. The Dalmatian pelican is the largest type of pelican. This pelican lives in Europe and Asia. Its wingspan is about 10 feet (3 m) long. Dalmatian pelicans are grayish white and the tips of their wings are black. They have feathers on their heads, and their pouches are orange or yellow.

There are not many Dalmatian pelicans left in the world because they are losing their wetland habitat. Without their habitat, pelicans cannot have new babies. Some people, though, are working to help save the wetland habitat for Dalmatian pelicans and other birds.

The Dalmatian pelican is sometimes called the curly-headed pelican. This is because the Dalmatian pelican has a group of curly feathers on the top of its head.

It's a Pelican's World

Pelicans are important birds. In some countries, fishermen use pelicans to help them find fish. When fishermen see pelicans flying, the fishermen know that fish are nearby.

Many pelicans are in danger, but there are things you can do to help. You can help pelicans by cleaning up a beach. You can do this with your family or with your class at school. Clean beaches are important. If pelicans eat trash that people leave on beaches, the pelicans may get sick. The best way to make sure pelicans can be around for a long time is to keep our world clean!

currents (KUR-ents) Air that flows in one direction.

drains (DRAYNZ) Lessens the amount of something.

female (FEE-mayl) Having to do with women and girls.

habitats (HA-beh-tats) The kinds of land where an animal or a plant naturally lives.

hatch (HACH) To come out of an egg.

male (MAYL) Having to do with men and boys.

polluted (puh-LOOT-ed) Hurt with certain kinds of bad matter.

predators (PREH-duh-terz) Animals that kill other animals for food.

shallow (SHA-loh) Not deep.

shrimp (SHRIMP) A small fish with a shell, a pair of claws, and a long tail.

soaring (SOR-ing) Flying very high in the air.

swamps (SWOMPS) Wetlands with a lot of trees and bushes.

wetlands (WET-landz) Land with a lot of moisture in the soil.

INDEX

WEB SITES

Due to the changing nature of Internet links, PowerKids
Press has developed an online list of Web sites related
to the subject of this book. This site is updated regularly.
Please use this link to access the list:
www.powerkidslinks.com/wings/pelican/

24